A GREAT NATION IS POSSIBLE

my nigerian dream

OSONDU CHILAGOR

authorHOUSE®

AuthorHouse™
1663 Liberty Drive
Bloomington, IN 47403
www.authorhouse.com
Phone: 1 (800) 839-8640

Published by AuthorHouse 03/15/2019

ISBN: 978-1-7283-0032-0 (sc)
ISBN: 978-1-7283-0031-3 (e)

Print information available on the last page.

Contact Information: Nigeria: **+234 (0) 803 618 1037, (0) 909 430 0700**

Dedication

This work is dedicated to my amiable boss, the indefatigable Dr (Mrs.) Adaora Umeoji Nwokoye – Deputy Managing Director Zenith Bank Plc., for her steadfast, unrelenting but quiet efforts at nation building which must not go unnoticed. You have become a bastion of hope for your generation.

To my father, Chief James Chilagor Chima – who is a man of integrity and who did his best to raise me up that way.

Foreword

"A Great Nation is Possible: *My Nigerian Dream"* represents a bold and daring attempt at correctly diagnosing a sick nation, convulsing and choking under the weight of its self-inflicted indulgence while recommending appropriate remedy in a manner that truly inspires hope.

The undeniably contagious hope seen through the lens of this great Nigerian Osondu Chilagor in the midst of our immanently uninspiring, negative existential circumstances readily interrogates the very essence of our belief in nationhood and the promises it should bring.

As a leadership expert of over twenty years, I cannot hide my fascination for his treatment of themes like Patriotism, Anti-Corruption, Moral Regeneration, Integrity, Accountability in leadership and so on.

Over the years, these areas have remained the bane of our challenges as a viable nation. Osondu literally navigated these issues with an uncanniness that is uniquely patriotic and practically dragged us into the center of his thoughts, dreams and world with persuasive optimism and creative passion.

I recommend this book to all Nigerians and indeed all those who pursue the noble cause of nation-building most times in their little unnoticed efforts. No doubt the contents of this book are ageless, defying time and space but poignantly expressing promise and unshaken confidence that a great Nigerian Nation is truly possible. This may be the most important book you will read this year!

Linus Okorie
President Guardian Of The Nation International (GOTNI),
Abuja – Nigeria.

Acknowledgments

I acknowledge the efforts of my beautiful wife Susan – my encourager-in-chief as well as critic; and also my lovely children – Amara, Deraa and Chima who see me as a great dad. Their support and love made this book possible. How can I forget our many reading and story-telling sessions?

I appreciate the hope, faith and prayers of a great number of Nigerians who still believe in a great Nigerian nation and have continued to prepare their hearts for her emergence.

My deep regards go to Dr Andy Osakwe and wife Pastor Ndidi for igniting conversations geared towards Nation building and for insisting everyone plays their part. I'm glad you agreed to go through this manuscript in spite of your busy schedule. Your support has been as constant as the Northern star.

I will not fail to acknowledge the support of Alhaji Abba Abdulkadir Kaka – a great and detribalized Nigerian whose steadfast encouragement has helped tremendously in making this work a reality.

Finally, I thank the Holy Spirit – my source, my strength and sustainer for birthing this inspiration and as always gracing my efforts to fruition.

Table of Contents

---◆◆---

Introduction

————◆◆◆————

A GREAT NATION IS POSSIBLE: My Nigerian Dream.

It is nearly a herculean task at this stage of our national development to inspire hope. There is virtually a potent sense of despair all around that we could literally slice through. It is not the sense of despair that troubles me; at least, I must admit we've been at stages like this - need i say worse moments than this many times before in our political evolution. However, there is the deafening suspense and silence over the possibility that the change experiment we tried and gave overwhelming support may be failing and dissipating our unbridled expectation. Or how else do we put it? That a nation in doldrums for the better part of five decades, now wants her "fantastic corruption", institutional failure, lack of patriotism all cured by one magical wand from her taciturn leader holding on to his avowed integrity but in a battle not just against age but the age of his ideas.

Honestly, such is the fallacy of expectation from what ordinarily we could refer to as an apprentice administration made up of a coalition of opportunistic forces that needed to test the complex waters of managing such a diverse, heterogeneous country. At least they have to move from mere theoretical idealization of their political campaign promises to concrete implementation of actions or blueprint if any.

This is where there is a disconnect. If we concede that what they saw from the comfort of their homes and the cheering of their teaming supporters on campaign grounds across the country is far different from the rot and decay they now see and I dare say – preside over, was there a perception problem? Despite the modest gains in terms of taming the security threat of Boko Haram and the fight against corruption, there are still a litany of security challenges including those that past governments have substantially managed.

The government now faces the challenges of armed herdsmen scouting for grazing land for their exhausted cattle while clashing with impetuous farmers leading to decimation of hitherto peaceful agrarian communities making the land a field of blood with its attendant toll on food production and security. The new low has also been the resurgence of militancy in the Niger delta creeks, kidnappings, killings and the seeming lack of value for human life. This militancy has its toll on oil production and earnings. There is also the attendant gas disruptions that has reduced the entire country to a "generator republic". The implication is first the paucity of funds for all levels of government to share, to pay salaries let alone embark on developmental projects. The nation is literally living on the edge. Although this administration has demonstrated great resolve in managing this, the latest security shame has been that of armed banditry and the human carnage in mind blowing proportions in Zamfara State, Birnin Gwari in Kaduna State as well as other adjoining States.

The fall to this despicable level one could

say was fairly predictable many years before now particularly if we consider the voracious and systematic culture of corruption that the Nigerian state adopted. The mono-economy that we lazily but gleefully practiced has cast us in the role of failing state without a blueprint for her own survival let alone a coherent economic policy. Could it be that no one saw this danger? No one made a patriotic call to warn of the impact to the now-generation and the generations unborn? Do we even have statesmen? Or is it a fact that we now live in a post-patriotic Nigeria?

The humongous entity we refer to as the Federal Republic of Nigeria must have been rid of its moral soul by her rapacious children who ruled and ruined her. Now we are hanging on the precipice wondering what has happened to us! The failing economy, evidenced by the free falling Naira and the weakened earning power coupled with the increased pump price for the petrol and the near erosion of the disposable income of the working class are proof positive of our unplanned nationhood. The army of unemployed youths surging – looking for jobs that are not there and the almost absence of infrastructure to support private enterprises is terrifying. Just as it is unbelievable for a nation that enjoyed so much oil wealth down the decades but refused or was unwilling to invest in her future and the future of her children.

Several decades ago, after the first military coup in January 15, 1966, Major Chukwuma Kaduna Nzeogwu in a broadcast captured the state of the Nigeria nation in this way:

"Our enemies are the political profiteers, the swindlers, the men in high and low places that seek bribes and demands ten percent, those that seek to keep the country divided permanently so that they can remain in office as ministers, VIPs at least; the tribalists, the nepotists, those that make the country look big for nothing before international circles, those that have corrupted our society and put Nigerian political calendar back by their words and deeds."[1]

Does this revolutionary rhetoric given more than fifty years ago strike a familiar chord in you? Even the coup speeches of Gen. Abacha in 1983 and some others harped on corruption and mismanagement of the economy as the reason for their "patriotic incursion" even though we now know better.

It is interesting to note that underlying all of these is the fact that our great nation has for the most part been headed dangerously towards a cliff with grave uncertainties. Also germaine is the fact that there has been interventions each time we go through these near calamitous experiences mostly from the self-proclaimed plotter – nationalists even when some of their interventions and solutions become an even more graver burden to the nation. Has there been responses from the political class, trade unions, civil society organizations and other non-state actors? Of course, apart from the politicians who create these problems themselves, there has been feeble or in some cases frightened responses from other stakeholders who believe the nation deserves better and should be rescued from the doldrums.

It is easy to see from this dialectical interaction of forces within the Nigeria political space from those who create the mess, then later to those-self-appointed to clean up the mess and thereafter end up a greater mess themselves, that there is a strong affinity. This strong affinity has a hue of nervous and untutored patriotism to engender national greatness. Such a greatness that protects the individual differences of ethnic nationalities. It was and still is a kind of greatness that our present elite, political, economic, military and even traditional leadership are yet to rise up to. The broadminded leadership that protects the majority interests but yet considers the interests of minorities not inclined to one's persuasion.

A particular period in our nationhood is particularly instructive in that it ushered in albeit strongly the issue of citizen's voice and resistance. The post annulment events of 1993 represents a watershed in our chequered political history as it brought to the fore the element of citizen resistance and action in the entrenchment of purpose in the nation. It bears repetition that before now, it's been the rhythmic transition between the "spoilers" and the "interventionists". The post annulment events witnessed the maturing of the citizens' will. Citizens transited from complaining in whispers, grumbling in the kitchens and drinking places to exploring their democratic rights of asking their leadership questions and holding them into account. Even the barrels of the gun succumbed to this sheer force of determined change leading to the eclipse of the Babangida administration. A new chapter was therefore opened in the quest for a great nation by the citizens' themselves who in my opinion should now drive the process.

The purpose of this book -'A Great Nation is Possible: My Nigerian Dream' is to create objective, fundamental grounds for the enthronement of a virile Nigerian nation state. These grounds are time-tested, universally acclaimed "ingredients" of success that can be relied upon as cornerstones to build an edifice that will stand the test of time. They are what every Nigerian can relate to and they are tribe-neutral, religion-neutral, language-neutral but value-laden capable of building the moral architecture of a nation in dire need of convictions.

These fundamental grounds can help reinforce the Nigerianess in us while providing rallying points on the basis of values, common purpose and destiny; common wealth and shared human and material resources to build the Nigeria of our dreams far beyond what the nationalists envisaged or dared to dream. Some of these fundamental ingredients are: Patriotism, Moral Regeneration, Integrity, Tolerance, Anti-Corruption, Followership and Accountability in leadership. In the subsequent chapters of this book, we will be considering them and their roles as catalysts in making a great nation possible!

Osondu Chilagor
Abuja – Nigeria.

---

[1] Major Nzeogwu's Speech announcing Nigeria's first coup (circa noon; January 15. 1966, Radio Kaduna)

Chapter ONE

What About Patriotism?

---◆◆◆---

Locked up inside me

Is a universe of ideas

Bursting forth...

Only for my nation.

– Osondu Chilagor

The quest to build a great nation is the cardinal objective of this work. A cursory look at the Nigeria society today reveals a lot of despair, lack of commitment to nation-building and even sometimes outright sabotage of our national interest on the altar of greed, selfishness, lack of patriotism, nepotism and so on.

The question arises: what is patriotism?

Patriotism has been severally defined by different authorities as primarily love, devotion, for one's country and willingness to sacrifice for it. These underlying qualities go to suggest that patriotism is not a light expectation for all citizens.

At the inaugural episode of my radio programme dubbed 'The nation Builders Forum', I had a guest, a young lawyer – Ocholi Okutepa who described patriotism summarily in terms of respect and love for one's nation. Respect in terms of acknowledging the rich history of the Nigeria nation and the labour of our heroes past. Recognizing the sacrifices of the nationalists and every such individual that played one definitive role or the other in making sure the foundation of a great nation is laid and a purposeful and destined nation is birthed. He believes that patriotism is first rooted in that reflective respect. He also believes patriotism should be rooted in love- unwavering and unconditional love for one's nation. For him, love for one's nation presupposes an acceptance of the now and future destiny of the nation. That ravishing passion to wish and work for the best for her. Accepting that common shared destiny between oneself and country whilst taking up responsibility for the building and establishment of the nation.

The import of Ocholi's perspective on patriotism should not be lost on us. I totally agree that there is a delicate connection between respect for the history of any nation for that matter and love for her present and future. Let's dig further. The respect he talks about doesn't necessarily mean the hallowed, deifying, and unquestioning servitude as of course every nation has its fair share of the ominous past-something regrettable, a sour point reflected in some nations as apartheid, in others as racism, in some others as institutional injustice, violence or indeed a combination of all or most of them. The respect stems out of the abiding understanding that every nation is in development. That while we take historical note of the 'shame' of the past or even the present, we respect our nation all the same with the determined focus on the evolution of our nation to that written down in our national anthem, pledge and etched in our dreams!

This respect should reflect in our regard for laws, national symbols, historical days and sites and i dare say an absolute respect for our shared history.

Loving one's nation in the human sense literarily means to consciously appreciate and treasure what we have and who we are. There are no methods or approach to doing this. Love always. Look for reasons and truly speaking these reasons are not in short supply in Nigeria's vast land.

You could start by loving her people-the sheer numbers that make us both the strength and dread of our world: and the quality of our human capital. The fact that the best brains, inventors, administrators, literary giants are all found in Nigeria. You could love the heterogeneity of her tribes and languages. Our languages are so exciting and rhythmic in its sounding. What about our land and water mass? The Niger and the Benue? How about our beautiful hills and valleys? Now talk about our clement weather-the rainforest and the savannahs? What about our exotic cultures and music? Virtually every known culture in Nigeria has a musical flair- a testimony of a perpetually grateful, jubilant and contented lifestyle. These can easily inspire patriotism. We are in harmony with nature wherever we are found.

It is easy to see that patriotism ought not to be from compulsion or force but from the abiding love and respect we have for our nation. This imposes a task on the present leadership and generation to make much and all of our history known to the emerging generation. Our schools should have in the curriculum the history of Nigeria: the beauty of our people; the sweetness of our waters, the valour of our warriors, the unimpeachable intellect of our scholars; the eloquence of our orators; the wisdom of our kings, the strength of our women; the creativity and passion of our youths; the vision of our founding fathers; the energy and dedication of our workers; the character of our families; the patience of our mothers; the discipline of our armed forces and the resolve and resilience of our entrepreneurs. When all of these are done, patriotism becomes a natural response from citizens.

We need to live out the well-crafted words of

our national anthem and pledge. We also need to re-ignite the nationalistic fervor in our lives again and quit this erroneous thinking that we now live in a post-patriotic Nigeria. Although much of what fuels this attitude is the sense of loss that a nation as blessed and advantaged as Nigeria has failed and continue to fail in her obligation to her citizens. It might be more correct to say the country because of the collapse and absence of its institutional structures rightly attributable to prolonged failure of leadership has been unable to justifiably discharge her duty of care to her teeming citizens thereby causing aspersions to be cast – one of which is lack of commitment to the goal of nationhood, and lack of confidence in the nation and her ability to protect the interests of disappointed citizens.

This lack of patriotism, however justifiable ought to be laid side in the interest of greater growth, since in the first instance, the sloppy state of the nation was inflicted by thieving, corrupt, visionless and narrow-minded leaders. It will take an equally positive energy from focused, patriotic and visionary leaders to fix the country hence the ardent call for patriotism.

Do you know that the greatness of any nation did not come by chance or accident; whether we are making reference to the greatness of countries like America, Britain, Japan or the ascendency of countries like China, India, Turkey, Malaysia or any other country under the sun? It came by a great sense of patriotism from citizens of those nations, respect for laws, love for country, its culture and the willingness to sacrifice and defend her institutions and shared values. Do you honestly believe that the present state of our nation represents the dreams and desires of our founding fathers?

Have you and I truly added value to the cause our founding fathers like Herbert Macaulay, Nnamdi Azikiwe, Ahmadu Bello, Obafemi Awolowo, Anthony Enahoro, Michael Okpara lived and died for? We need a new Nigeria, a Nigeria known for greatness. This therefore is a clarion call for patriotic action from all citizens. What do I do to make her great?

Chapter **TWO**

The Moral Regeneration Call

—◆—◆—

In this marriage of pragmatism and capitalism,

Where lies our values?

In this quest for profit,

Do you hurt your neighbour?

– Osondu Chilagor

There is an absolute need for the reworking of our ethical framework and value-system. The seeming lack of boundaries or lack of consensus on what is considered a generally accepted behavior has been our albatross as a society.

Every human society has its own sets of do's and don'ts – written or unwritten that is delicately and systematically built into her culture and worldview. Deviations from such acceptable norms of behavior are considered outlandish and strange.

This explains why Albert Schweitzer a German philosopher wrote that "A civilization that develops only on its material side and not in corresponding measure in the sphere of the spirit is like a ship with defective steering gear which gets out of control at a constantly accelerating pace and thereby heads for catastrophe."[2]

However we view the issue of moral regeneration, it is obviously the basis for any meaningful progress in society. To put it in clear terms, without our value systems, we can only prepare for doom because as Schweitzer puts it: "The more we build, the greater the ruins."[3] There is therefore this saying that "the prosperity of any society depends on the moral disposition of its members."[4]

The task for building a great Nigeria nation will be easier if there is a universal basis for accepting morality and moral standards. In this case, it does hold true that "morality has its roots in the rational and social nature of man.

If man were not a rational being, or if he were not a social being, there would be no such thing as morality."[5]

Considering also the universality of the human nature and rationality, it is therefore possible to have a consensus on what is considered appropriate behavior; what is considered acceptable and on the contrary what is viewed as repugnant across cultures, languages and religions. It is important that I lay these foundations so that the call for moral regeneration in Nigeria will be understood, accepted and heeded. "Moral principles are explicit formulations of the moral law. They are by their nature universal, that is they are valid and applicable at all times in all societies."[6]

Moral principles are actually abstractions from the law. These principles could be positive in that they encourage the cultivation of values like hospitality, trust, love kindness… and they could be negative in that they prohibit certain actions or vices which ought to be avoided. The moral principles also aim at preserving values ultimately sourced from the moral law. The moral law for instance frowns at killing a fellow human being, stealing, corruption and it is the duty of the principles of morality to uphold these.

A lot of times, it is easy to ignore the question: why should I be moral or why should there be a moral regeneration in Nigeria. Despite the strident calls for change in ethical orientation as most governments in the past have championed, there is the evident lack of support or lack of understanding from citizens and even more painfully the government driving such programme as it fails to secure the buy-in of citizens. Most times, as a people or as a country, we are pre-occupied with certain actions not minding the moral implications of such actions. Professor Nkeonye Otakpor observes that "the just man is happy because his soul is harmoniously ordered. He has an integrated personality and the unjust corrupt man's personality is disintegrated and his soul is a chaos of internal strife."[7]

By extension, a just society or a society that seeks and pursues justice will always be harmoniously ordered, integrated and prosperous. We might wish to predicate the need for moral regeneration in Nigeria on the foundation of this marriage of necessity between rationality and nature. It may be correct to say nature ensures and enforces natural harmony and my rationality based on this premise begins instructively and instinctively to tell me that:

1. If I commit murder, I violate nature's law by making somebody childless, fatherless, a widower or a widow.

2. If I commit adultery, it will be immoral and a case of breach of trust or fidelity.

3. If I steal, I dispossess somebody of his/her prized possession or render him poor which is bad.

4. If I vandalize the school's facilities, I end up destroying what was reserved for me by others who graduated before me which is morally wrong.

5. If I, in anyway, distort, obstruct, or set in disequilibrium the course of nature, I am bound to be judged by the laws since I am a constituting part of nature.

Other generally accepted positions why one should be moral are:

1. Because of God: this view is tied to religious belief.

2. The golden rule: the rule holds that I (or any other person) should not do unto others what I wouldn't like done to me

3. The law of Nemesis: a lot of people live their moral lives in conscious avoidance of the law of nemesis. Sometimes this view is regarded as the law of karma or retribution – that is punishment for offenses committed before.

Apart from the above reasons for being moral, there is need for commitment to moral principles. There is no doubting the fact that morality is the foundation of all essential elements of any enduring human civilization as we know it, whether we are talking about the ancient Greeks or the contemporary Nigerian situation. In a lecture delivered in November 1994 in Hillsdale College, Michigan, Margaret Thatcher former British Prime Minister spoke about the moral foundation of societies. She makes many emphatic claims about the moral basis of sustainable human civilization. She points out, for example the moral foundations of the law, the moral foundation of capitalism, she explains what happens to any society, ancient, modern or contemporary that has to ignore commitment to moral principle such as human freedom.

According to her, "the Athenian society collapsed because it wanted security, comfort and freedom. This was because the freedom it was seeking was freedom from responsibility."[8] She explains further how this lack of moral commitment in our time deprives many nations of economic growth. In terms of natural resources Russia is one of the richest countries in the world. And so Nigeria, she asks, why isn't Russia the wealthiest country in the world? Why aren't resources rich countries in the third-world at the top of the list? It is because their governments deny citizens their God-given rights and talents.

The point being made is that morality is at the heart of the growth and development of any human civilization. Nigeria is no exception. In order to grow politically, socially, economically and in every wise, the basic claim here is that Nigerians or any other group for that matter must be committed to sound moral principles. I am here boldly challenging anybody who tries to claim that success, efficiency, improved productivity, high performance in our social life must of necessity be inhuman and unethical.

The issue of success, efficiency, improved productivity, high performance should no longer be separated from relevant ethical consideration. We have to redefine these key concepts within the context of their human origin to incorporate the ethical without which there can be no real sustainable civilization. We have to stop pretending that the injustice we do to others is deserved by them. We cannot continue to pretend to be happy knowing that what we are doing is morally wrong. The real issue is not whether or not we can get away with doing evil, whether or not there is a godfather somewhere up there who will guarantee us legal protection or complete immunity against prosecution or punishment if discovered.

The real issue is that we must accept it as a guiding principle that there are right and wrong ways of conducting one's life and doing things and that it pays to be morally good. There is a stringent demand that we live the morally good life- a demand that is neither arbitrary nor a matter of personal opinion but rather something that arises from some abiding principles in man's own nature.

In closing this chapter, we shouldn't lose sight of the fact that it is a difficult task to have a water tight moral consensus that will not become vulnerable to the risk of being obsolete with changing times particularly in a dynamic society like ours. Also, one more reason proffering an acceptable morality has repeatedly failed in Nigeria is the attendant suspicion that a group or select elite are in subtle and seemingly harmless way attempting to foist their personal views of morality on the generality of the people thus all actions in this regard are viewed as one shrouded with peevish intent and content.

---

[2] A. O. Schweitzer; Civilization and Ethics (N. P. Unwin Books 1961), p.20

[3] U. G. Ukagba; Lecture Note on Ethics, 2001, Unpublished, University of Benin, 1999/2000 Academic Year

4 A. O. Schweitzer; Civilization and Ethics (N. P. Unwin Books 1961), p.76

5 J. Omoregbe, Ethics, A Systematic and Historical Study (Lagos Joja Publishers Ltd, 1993), p.150

6 J. Omoregbe, Ethics, A Systematic and Historical Study (Lagos Joja Publishers Ltd, 1993), p.150

7 N. Otakpor; The Moral Crisis in Nigeria (Enugu: Delta Publications Ltd, 2000), p.8

8 C. S. Nwodo "Political Stability and Social Well-being in Aristotile's Political Philosophy: Its Relevance to the Nigerian Situation. Africa Philosophy and Public Affairs (ed) O. Oguejiofor, Enugu: Delta Publication, 1998, p.72 – 73

Chapter THREE

What About Integrity?

A nation founded on truth

Where oppression is far

And justice is served

Is the nation we build.

– Osondu Chilagor

Integrity is what it is! A certain truthfulness to oneself. Some may tag it as trustworthiness or dependability. Integrity could also be seen as the consistency of thoughts, convictions and actual actions. A kind of congruence between normative beliefs; its interpretation and actions.

A nation of integrity is simply one whose citizens ride high on their personal integrity.

Of course when we talk about integrity, we do not forget the individual's worldview, his environment and the normative laws that rule his universe. Some or all of these existential factors help in building the individual's convictions which in turn affects the community, society and social order that becomes prevalent.

One of my bosses, a Deputy Managing Director told a large gathering of bank executives the Emperor's seed story some years ago. How a certain Chinese emperor who was childless and needed to choose an heir decided to give thousands of children across his kingdom seeds to go to their villages, provinces and plant and nurture for one year. The emperor would eventually judge their efforts and choose his successor.

The summary of the story she told was that at the end of one year, thousands of kids showed up before the emperor with shrubs, leafy trees, all manner of beautiful trees as a testimony of their stewardship and suitability for the throne except Ling.

Ling has been mocked, jeered by other kids

for not having any results after watering his own seed daily with the mother's help. Don't take anything from Ling: he has been dedicated, forthright, hardworking, and enthusiastic as he patiently watered his seed pot every day. This seems to be the sour point in integrity – sometimes there is a certain aloneness you will feel in not joining the band wagon. You really have to be steadfast and rise up within to the crowd mentality as it dares to annex or swallow up your convictions. At those moments one must be willing to stand alone, endure the isolation and social alienation. Ling endured all these and remained steadfast.

The emperor inspected thousands of pots to see grown trees, leafy stems, shady shrubs but never stopped until he got to ling's empty and barren pot. Another round of jeering and mockery rent the air again but the emperor knew better. He called up Ling and announced to the amazement of the multitude that a year ago he gave all the kids boiled seeds – incapable of ever growing again and now only Ling has demonstrated true integrity not minding the back lash he could get.

The emperor promptly named Ling as his successor while emphasizing that integrity and courage are more important values for leadership than proud displays.

The learning point here is simple: personal integrity might not be convenient but it is necessary if one is to live a worthy life. The ingredient of integrity is so vital that it separates men and women of honor from villains. Personal integrity easily snowballs into business and organizational integrity. What a transformation this can bring to our nation Nigeria!

There is another fascinating example of personal integrity that I wish to share which relates to one of my bosses. This case is actually a locus-classicus and well documented in that it brought much honour to Nigeria and Nigerians in South Africa and even earned my boss – Gabriel Okenwa the nation's national award. Permit me to share this story briefly. Mr Okenwa who was a Banker by profession while on a visit to the country had gone to a bank to carry out a financial transaction. He was overpaid by a cashier a huge amount and could easily like many others blessed his good fortune and bolted away. He did none of that but instead returned the over-payment much to the astonishment of the South Africans.

There is a reason I am using an example that happened in our day and age which could also apply to our own circumstances. It is indeed very easy to follow the escapist path by saying 'well, that was then not now'. But truly, integrity, be it personal or institutional is important and essential for all times, all races, all socio-political and economic circumstances. Of course any nation whose citizens adopt personal and institutional integrity is bound to succeed in every sphere of human endeavour and will enjoy prosperity.

Several years ago as a young lad, I could remember asking my dad – now a septuagenarian – why it appeared to me that dubious people, tricksters, seem to be doing well in terms of having material advantage. Mind you, this picture of mine was reinforced upon close observation of my dad – a hardworking factory supervisor who was so dedicated – he wouldn't miss a day at work under any pretence. It didn't seem to me he was better off materially compared to some others in his office who could scheme, cheat and yet show much considerable resources. It presented itself as a big contradiction in my forming and hazy mind then. But then, my father's wise and timeless counsel that a good name is better than silver and gold has helped me understand better and benefitted me immensely in my adult life.

The pictures seem so clear now that when I look at my dad now alongside his contemporaries who did engage in sharp practices ten-twenty years down the line, a lot of them have one bitter story or the other to tell and quite a lot are lost in the social radar. The advantage, the materials, the ill-gotten wealth seemed to evaporate. It wasn't sustainable and enduring and to make matters worse, it did leave them with scars of a bad name.

Meanwhile, my dad after thirty years of meritorious service to his organization and nearly fifteen years of exiting it has remained a major contractor to the organization – a reward that only personal integrity and forthrightness would have earned him.

It is true our national and personal histories are littered with cases of an abject lack of integrity which has become our albatross as a nation hindering us from being the kind of nation we ought to be. Chinua Achebe, Africa's foremost novelist once said that we should know from where the rains started beating us if we are to make an informed change. It is never too late to adopt a life of integrity as a nation. As a matter of fact, once we follow the path of honour we are going to witness the kind of transformation that is truly mind-blowing and help us create a nation of possibilities.

Chapter **FOUR**

Corruption: The Enemy of a Secure Society

---◆◆◆---

Life steals from the corrupt,

Providence cheats the greedy,

Posterity robs the crooked,

History annihilates their legacy.

– Osondu Chilagor

The fundamental question as always is 'what is Corruption'? I understand not a few people will be bored at hearing the word corruption. This is understandably so because the subject is the most talked about either from our bedrooms, kitchens, places of worship, schools, offices, political party meetings and gatherings of social relevance. The issue of corruption occupies the central place of discourse. One may even safely assume that consensus building is easily achieved whenever and wherever Nigerians discuss on the subject of corruption.

According to Transparency International, corruption is the abuse of entrusted power for private gain. It hurts everyone who depends on the integrity of the people in the position of authority. Apart from this definition of corruption, there are still those who believe that corruption is a spiritual and psychological challenge. This school of thought holds that corruption which when used as an adjective means "utterly broken" is first and foremost a spiritual or mental challenge fuelled by uncontrolled greed, materialism and a desire to hold more than is necessary. Although there are external factors that encourage corruption such as the level of poverty, poor remuneration, unemployment and even under-employment, it is easy to understand that corruption in our land and clime has to do with both internal and external factors. It is important that I concede that it is almost practically impossible to exhaust the topic as broad and ageless as corruption.

From prehistoric times, there is actually no nation or society that has completely rid itself of this menace called corruption. It is equally noteworthy to consider the danger of such a monster particularly in a society like ours where it thrives on such a colossal scale. Now the question is, where did it all go wrong?

A few years ago, I had a guest in our radio programme – Mr Clem Betseh who expressed a bit of hesitation at giving a direct definition of corruption. I could understand his dilemma as he voiced the fact that corruption means different things to different people. Everyone is quick to say that the problem of Nigeria is corruption. The governors, contractors, legislators, the market women, the labour unions and the man on the street. There is the well-rehearsed finger-pointing of corruption as though it is external to us. It appears as though we are here, and corruption is somewhere there encroaching and eating up all of our human space. How self –absolving!

My guest eventually settled for a broad definition of corruption as knowing what is right but choosing to do what is wrong. Smart enough to involve every finger-pointing and self-absolving citizen!

Our other-worldly treatment of corruption has been the reason for our failure to deal with this menace and its tragic consequences in our lives and the life of our nation. Our narrow-minded perception of corruption has not helped matters at all. The practice of corruption is not only in looting of the public treasury and commonwealth. It is far more! Its scope and far reaching effects permeates our daily lives. For instance, if one steals 'not-for-sale-drugs' from the public hospital and sell it outside for pecuniary gains, such a person is stewing in corruption. If one signs up for a job, and choose not to do it while taking the benefits, the person is corrupt. If one tampers with his or her age to gain advantage over others, the person is engaging in corruption.

If a lecturer has courses to teach for which he or she is paid and doesn't do it but still examine students inspite of the lack of commitment, the lecturer is corrupt. If a pump attendant collects the right money while still under-dispensing fuel or any product to unsuspecting customers, such a fellow is corrupt.

The brand of exploitative capitalism we practice in our country somehow legitimizes corruption. The capitalism that places profit before people, practically draining their human worth, completely ostracizing them from goods they produce, denying or giving them limited welfare while dumping them when no longer useful can also be seen as corruption. Even the bible in James 5:4 speaks vehemently against the negative practices of capitalism as corruption.

I sense I might have burst a few bubbles in my new perspective interpretation of corruption that makes us see the problem of corruption as wholly ours and here rather than 'theirs' and 'there'. Corruption is not just an abstract phenomenon. It represents a character flaw and behavioral deficiency.

Clem goes further to say that corruption should not be merely narrowed down to financial impropriety or some random government official looting the treasury and I cannot agree less.

The corruption menace seems to me like expressions of a twisted worldview, a derailed nationalism and an incensed and contagious perversion. Only a worldview adjustment, a deliberate value reorientation can produce possible remedy. Of course, our national corruption mess is uniquely psychopathic, depressing and could even more require a bit of mental re-examination and guided counseling to let citizens understand there is no need to steal what one cannot even spend and exhaust in ten life times! Humorous isn't it? In fact, there is no need to steal at all.

J. S. Mbiti a scholar once said 'I am because you are, because you are, therefore I am'. This statement is reflective of a communal society with strong bond, brotherliness, contentment, neighbourliness with commitment to progress. All these are the values, corruption now destroys.

Growing up, I remember been told by my parents and grandparents alike that a good name is better than riches. This sense of nostalgia only goes to register in my consciousness that for us to have a corruption free society, we must have good homes. Society must place emphasis on what truly matters. These craze and crave for unjust and unearned gain must stop particularly when it is ripped off the people's commonwealth. It is criminal just as it is wicked and immoral.

Why do people mindlessly steal particularly when in a position of trust? Is it to show off their social status, or image? I think it is better to build a buoyant, just and prosperous society than to own personal fortune. I recall a cartoon I saw in the dailies many years ago where certain characters were used to depict the growth, progress and problem of corruption in our society. A certain character in the cartoon said quite humorously with a lean cheek 'I stole in tens'; another character somewhat in the seventies said 'I stole in thousands' while in the eighties – another character said 'I stole in millions'. The last character-obviously with a robust cheek was audacious enough to say 'I stole in billions'. These comical representations depict the stages and growth of corruption in the society, from the sixties, seventies, eighties, down to the present day Nigeria. Should this continue unchecked?

There is so much talk about having an appropriate legal framework that is firm enough to secure 'quick' convictions for the supposedly corrupt as those who indulge in corruption seem to be having a field day exploiting technicalities within our legal jurisprudence to get off the hook, after long, unfruitful legal process spanning years.

There is the imminent danger that evidence becomes inadmissible and certain star witnesses die or are no longer there to corroborate their initial testimonies.

Can we possibly forget several cases of lack of diligent prosecution by the prosecuting authority that eventually sees all charges thrown out after endless adjournments? The legal frame work as we have it today provides lots of loop holes for rich and elite offenders to dribble the law and evade convictions. In fact the not-so-lucky but connected offenders can sometimes land sentences that are at best a slap on the wrist while still enjoying all their loot.

Our institutional capacity to fight corruption remains suspect. It is personality-centered rather than institution-centered. This accounts for the hue and cry in certain quarters about selective prosecution of corruption cases as institutions set up to fight corruption are perceived as looking in certain directions while looking away from certain other directions. These are some of the reasons the fight against corruption is considered marred with the issue of subjective inwardness rather than systemic and systematic approach it requires.

Apart from the legal constraints, there is the environmental and social colouration. The Nigerian society as presently constituted today is one that admires, celebrates and idolizes corruption. The act of corruption is sadly viewed from ethnic and religious prisms. Our perceptions are intentionally perverted while making heroes and freedom fighters out of supposedly corrupt persons.

The traditional institutions fall over each other to give titles; town unions and professional bodies and lately the media has joined the fray brandishing all manners of phoney and laughable titles with none bothering about the source of wealth of the individual. All manner of unsubstantiated accomplishments are attributed to the individual just so that everyone gets a share of the filthy lucre- effectively laundering the image of the corrupt and making the practice of it a truly rewarding enterprise!

In closing, I think we need to go back to our values. This western individualization of me, myself and I that is so visible these days expressed in tall fences, lack of neighbourliness and lack of patriotism that has now obsessed us and creating the breeding ground for corruption must give way. We need to become persons who will relate with other persons in our society with a shared human and nationalistic spirit.

We need to feel the pulse and yearnings of other persons in the society. If we become our brothers' keeper, we won't loot as mindlessly as we do today. This will translate to good roads; functional hospitals well equipped schools; stable power and buoyant economy. It will also lead to a great Nigeria, secure, prosperous and full of opportunities for all.

Chapter FIVE

Accountability As A National Character

---◆-◆-◆---

The voyage of leadership

Is propelled by vision

Imbued with sacrifice – not for wayfarers.

Do you want to lead?

– Osondu Chilagor

What exactly does it mean to be accountable? What is the role of accountable leadership in building a virile and great nation? It is largely true that since the advent of our democratic journey in 1999, we have been practicing a brand of representative democracy where leaders of the people emerge from the people with their consent by way of periodic elections; although that refers to political leadership and indeed, there are other forms of leadership we have- be it professional, religious, trade union, economic leadership and so on.

Are these leaders accountable? Do they truly represent the people they are meant to serve? I had a guest on my radio programme some years ago, Rev. Victor Atokolo, a patriotic and passionate Nigerian, who shared his thoughts on accountability in leadership.

He sees accountability as the willingness to be held responsible for our actions and to have somebody else's mind interact with ours in deciding whether what one did was right or wrong. The willingness not to be the final authority. It is also the willingness to trust other people's intelligence to examine our own in the choices we have made. Very profound thoughts indeed!

Accountable leadership submits one's decisions or actions for oneself and that made for others to scrutiny. This involves a lot of humility and self-comportment. It hardly gives room for any form of arrogance. After all, the primary aim of leadership is service and the quality of service has to be determined by persons other than us. Since the call to leadership is the call to serve, then it absolutely matters that we get feedback as to the relevance, purposefulness and usefulness of our service. The people you lead should be permitted to examine the choices you make for them, whether it is moving them in the direction they want to go or not. If you are called to serve the people, you should be willing for their inputs to count for something.

A cursory look at our democratic leadership from 1999 shows that the political leadership hasn't shown or seen the need to be accountable. Infact, a lot of them have dismissed and worse still crushed opposition. Although people still view this intemperate, impatient and non-accommodative reaction to dissenting views as part of the evolution of our home grown democracy. Victor Atokolo thinks otherwise.

He actually enthused that accountability by the political class is never easily relinquished; it has to be demanded by citizens. According to him, when leaders realize they will not be permitted to lead without being accountable, they will increasingly become more and more accountable to win the people's followership.

It is important to state that our traditional leadership patterns have influenced accountability in political leadership albeit negatively. While not inferring that our traditional stools as they used to and presently exist are not accountable, we must note that across the spectrum from North to South, all of them enjoyed some sort of absolute and unimpeachable authority. They wielded and continue to wield unchallenged authority in domestic affairs, foreign policy and so on. It is very likely that we may have carried over this traditional pattern to our democracy.

Of course, the crop of leadership we have come from this same population with the traditional worldview who see their monarchy as an extension of God that cannot be questioned by mere mortals. This should explain why some of our governors behave like emperors and imperial majesties and ride rough shod over the people. This should also explain why it is difficult for them to surrender accountability. For our leadership to become more accountable, it is expedient that this overcast traditional patterns be whittled down by appropriate legislations. Our leaders are not unimpeachable or infallible and therefore should be accountable.

Even when we have appropriate legislations like the Freedom of Information Act of 2015, there is also a greater need to adjust our overtly cultural mindset of passive subservience to active democratic participation by demanding accountability through available legislative and legal vehicles. The traditional institutions should remain custodians of customs and traditions and not custodians of power. They cannot be said to be good models of accountability in a democracy.

There is this nexus between accountability and national development. Where we have a system that demands and breeds accountability and is intolerant of mediocre, self-effacing and indolent leaders, national development becomes the endpoint.

Considering where we are coming from in our democratic journey, it is important we are patient as our democratic systems evolves to throw up accountable leaders. This patience however cannot be forever. It's okay to draw comparisms between our leaders, our political systems with that of western democracies but we should recognize that these western democracies have come a long way. At some point, history records that some of them were brutish at their primitive best. They practiced subjugation and gleefully attacked personal liberties. The barbarism of the west and the revolts against its subversive and tyrannical instincts resulted in most cases in the overthrow of its monarchical system in Europe. The gruesome overthrow of the absolute monarchical systems was indeed largely due to the fact that they were not accountable and exercised powers without restraint. Even in countries like England and Spain where these monarchies still exist, they do so as relics of the past to remind those nations of their histories.

However, we can accelerate the process of having an accountable system that throws up accountable leaders when we demand it. The truth is that our leaders will always rise up to the kind of standards we set for them.

There is something amazing I have observed from history about despots and dictators, whether it be Benito Mussoloni, Idi Amin Dada, Adolf Hitler, Mobutu Sese Seko, Stalin, Sani Abacha, Moumer Ghadaffi, Hosni Munarak and the likes. It is the fact that most of them began with the most noble of ideas and showed great nationalistic fervour.

They championed liberation and some others supremacist ideologies for their people. They actually had their work cut out for them. Having risen up to heroic applause and approvals before their people, most of them failed in the end because there was no system of accountability to check them. They seemed to be above the system and above the law. They in most cases actually overreached themselves and seemed to be above scrutiny.

This caused them and the ideologies they passionately pursued to self-destruct. Their dynasties fell like a pack of cards leaving their beloved countries as ash heaps, reeling in despair and division decades later. Truth be told, I have come to the carefully considered view that it is better to be a weak leader in an accountable system than to be the most benevolent, charismatic, visionary and even enigmatic leader in a system marred with the dearth of accountability.

We must bring up a new generation of Nigerians to think accountability using the home grown approach. Men should be accountable to their wives and vice versa. How can a man challenge his Member of Parliament to be accountable where he himself don't feel obliged to be accountable to his family? Is it not to indulge in a contradiction of sorts?

There is nothing wrong in having national structures to enforce accountability but it is important that we build a culture of accountability in our personal lives, our small family units, our professional bodies and our peer group system. The sustained culture of transparency will help Nigeria consolidate its democratic reforms and make it the economic bride of Africa and the entire world.

When leadership across board - whether federal, states, local, judicial, legislative, economic or non-governmental – recognize and embrace accountability, they hit the right spot. The right spot being the people. The people that all forms of leadership is actually about. The history of leadership in Nigeria has largely been that of instability and lack of focus and because of this instability, the focus of the leadership became parochial with the overriding consideration for personal survival rather than national development. But all of these are changing in this new and great Nigeria we are building today as accountability permeates our social, political, economic, religious and cultural space. We are awakened to the new dawn of a great nation, secure prosperous, virile and the powerhouse of Africa.

Chapter SIX

The Followership Question

Green white green…

Green blessed green…

Green wise green…

Our arteries flow with majestic green blood!

– Osondu Chilagor

What the heck is followership? Is it as good and important as leadership? Followership is specifically the capacity of an individual to actively follow a leader. It is also the reciprocal social process of leadership. In our social and political space today, there is so much hue and cry about leadership-whether it meets our expectations or fails to meet our expectation and most of the time, we leave out the equally important part of leadership which is followership.

It actually does take a lot more to follow. For instance, interpreting a leader's vision; making it ours and running with it. There is a great level of harmonious cooperation of the human will to follow. This is what makes certain people see followership as passive, pedestrian, and I dare say weak!

On the contrary, it takes great strength to follow, to sometimes suspend personal judgment and align our actions. In a sense, it is an act of maturity and deep faith. For any democratic experiment to thrive there is need for this dialectical interaction between leadership and followership. There must be a strong connection-especially something of a causal relationship where both are constructively and cooperatively engaged.

Several years ago, as an undergraduate student of the University of Benin, I had this friend who is famed for saying that 'if you lead, and no one follows, you are merely taking a stroll.' So so true!

It is actually expected of focused leadership to carry the followers along; they must not be seen to go on a frolic of their own. In any case, since the leadership derives their legitimacy from citizen-followers, they ought to as a matter of covenant engage them. Very often across the world and in Nigeria, we experience vibrant, charismatic and visionary leadership that have lost followership. Even though one must admit, these leaderships might have the best of intentions and programmes, they tend to fail miserably.

Very central to the symbiotic engagement between leadership and followership must be 'the message'. People don't just desire leadership for its sake alone. There is something it is meant or expected to do. The constant communication or the successful accomplishment or otherwise of this expectation can safely be regarded as the message. To inspire active and enthusiastic followership, the message must be prompt, progressive and in line with the article of faith between leadership and followership.

Most times, it is at this level that this pivotal national relationship gets fragmented and the consequence: leadership goes on a stroll while followership becomes docile and uninvolved. These two evils are recipes for stagnated and retrogressive society.

In recent Nigeria history, there are about two examples where strong followership was demonstrated. The Jonathan election of 2011 and the Buhari election of 2015.

The Jonathan followership was fuelled largely by the sentiment that Nigeria has never had a president from the minorities and the oil producing areas. Given the nature of politics and nominations for flag bearers of political parties in Nigeria, it would seem very unlikely that a minority Ijaw would become President. But somehow, Goodluck Ebele Jonathan sold a passionate message that stuck with many. It would be difficult to forget that catch phrase 'I had no shoes'.

Across the country, his cult of followership was overwhelming just as he maximized his incumbency advantage. The roller-coaster relationship lasted until its first major strain in the January 2012 fuel subsidy protests. Because he couldn't sustain that message, it started going downhill for his acceptability and his presidency. Several allegations of corruption began to surface and because he failed to actively connect and resuscitate that vital followership relationship, it culminated in his failure at the 2015 presidential election.

The Buhari election of 2015 is still fresh on our minds. His cult of followership was actually mind boggling in the run up to the election. Only such could successfully unseat an incumbent and this he actually accomplished. However it is not difficult to reach the conclusion that his followership has begun to dwindle and evaporate.

Many still believe that he is a man of impeccable integrity, but is that enough? Following his delay to appoint ministers and several other government functionaries, and his unwillingness or is it inability at the time to treat the economy as a national emergency, he started losing ardent followership. Perhaps as can be observed now, the greatest undoing of his presidency is the handling and communication of government's information to his teeming followers, by this I mean Nigerians.

For instance, the conflicting, uncoordinated information on the subject of his health cost him several other followers. Also his handling of the herdsmen / farmers' issue leaves little to be desired; not to mention the now shameful and intractable fuel scarcity that reared its head at some point. No leadership is ever perfect and in the same vein, no followership demands perfection from leadership. In fact where the relationship is mutually respectful, cordial and sincere, there is guaranteed and committed followership.

It is often said that a leadership will always be as good as its followership. A great proportion of our failures and woes today are conveniently heaped on leadership either past or present. They take the blame for our infrastructure decay, they take the blame for insecurity in the land and failure of institutions. They even take the blame for our own inability to obey the traffic light!

To tell you how deep this runs, when there is

a family quarrel or street fight or when we fail to pay our tax or properly dispose our refuse- intentionally blocking the drainage, resulting in flood, we blame leadership also! Granted, leadership as it presents itself in our nation today cannot excuse itself from the rot we experience. However, it is equally correct to say that our greatest undoing as a nation today is that of bad followership.

From time to time during elections, we pick leaders from supposed followers yet the difference is not clear at all. It is followers who indulge and make bad leadership to thrive. If we choose to have bold, courageous, and supportive followership today and make it part of our political culture, what a great nation we will be!

Chapter **SEVEN**

Rethinking Our 'Nigerianess'

Oh the bliss of our temperate streams and rivers,

Our calm and resourceful hills and valleys.

Should I speak of our musical languages

Or the fertility of our land and people?

– Osondu Chilagor

We surely do live in interesting times indeed! This age of information that we find ourselves sometimes constrains us to demand answers to questions, widely accepted beliefs and dogmas, query ideologies and phenomena that could be regarded as absolutes.

It is in the light of this fact that having been regarded as a Nigerian all these years, one is inclined as a matter of self-appraisal to ask, who is a Nigerian?

Again I ask, are there attributes or behavioural traits that one can readily ascribe or uniquely describe as Nigerian? What exactly is the proper way to introduce ourselves? For instance, is it ideal to say I am an Ijaw man from Nigeria or I am a Nigerian of Ijaw extraction? Are they the same thing?

What should come first, allegiance to ethnic nationality, religious grouping or the nation? While our ethnic or tribal origins have largely shaped us, and played its role in our worldview, should they remain prisms from which we see and judge the rest of the world?

Some years ago, when I ran nation building series on radio, I had this interesting guest Mr. Nkem Anyata Lafia, Executive Assistant on Media to the Imo State Governor and Managing Editor Imo Today Newspaper. He was every inch a palace intellectual with a firm belief in project Nigeria. When I asked him the question who is a Nigerian? He had this to say:

"A Nigerian is somebody who has been born

in Nigeria or somebody who having been born in some other country, is now a naturalized person in Nigeria. Let me also say that a Nigerian is that person who likes to dare things. A Nigerian is that person who God has endowed with a lot of gifts- a Nigerian is that person who belongs to this country created by God with a lot of talents, so endowed that he or she can standout anywhere he is. We stand out in the field of medicine, sports, academics, arts, engineering and in every field of human endeavor."

Very interestingly, he added that "A Nigerian is that person who has the inner ability to withstand whatever pressure and to do things that the result will astound even the best of men in the whole world."

I find his description of a Nigerian incurably positive and reassuring. On the scale of truth-he is equally on point in spite of the pervasively negative tar Nigerians have been painted with by the rest of the world. The uncommon resolve and inner strength we have causes us to excel in practically any endeavour, positive or negative. Herein lies the problem: letting our Nigerianess reflect in positive energy, excellent attitude and an unquestionable integrity and never in condemnable behaviour and outlandish character.

Besides Anyata-Lafia's portrayal of Nigeria, there have been several seemingly remarkable expressions of our Nigerianess in works of art, music, industry, trade, sports and entertainment by individuals and corporations that have equally attracted worldwide acclaim.

Very recent on my mind was the tenacious campaign by one of our amazons; erudite scholar and accomplished administrator – the late Professor (Mrs) Dora Akunyili of blessed memory. The well thought out campaign she led and pursued vigorously rubbed off positively on our national psyche and spirit.

The campaign attempted to boost self-confidence and strengthen self-esteem with the well-articulated phrase 'good people, great nation'. There is indeed no better way to properly describe the nation and people of Nigeria without recourse to the indisputable fact that we are good and great! I make bold to say that the biggest problem and burden we have to cope with as a nation today is that of self-definition. What is the proper constitution of a Nigerian?

The passive acceptance of the colonial christening without any corresponding formulation of abiding and acceptable characteristics is an issue. In a lot of ways too, not defining who we are has led to many self-determination movements bedeviling our country today. People within the confines and safety of their ethnic and geographical groupings construct their clannish ideologies and then immediately see the inconsistencies within the largely undefined Nigerian characteristics and boom!

The result is an uneasiness, impatience, agitation and a sense of being in a claptrap in an uncultivated Nigerian project. If our leaders past or present, in strengthening the foundation of our nationhood devote a little more time in establishing an accommodating framework that shows our Nigerianess, then there is an appropriate model and mould to fashion the character of the nation into.

What that will do for us immediately is that we will essentially know and understand what is unNigerian. Now having known what it is to be Nigerian, our entire value systems, school curriculum, businesses, physical and moral architecture will be made to align with the Nigerian framework. A Nigerian framework that enforces unity in diversity need not be perfect if it does point in a clear progressive direction. Rather the constant evolution of life will consequently result in the utilitarian disposition of the framework through constant reworkings and reformulations.

It is clearly possible that there are naysayers (and truly there are) who believe the concept of Nigeria is a big lie and that the Lugard's amalgamation is an accident of history. As much as I sympathise and respect this school of thought, I confidently believe it is symptomic of a great nation that has refused to understand its identity or discover herself.

Agitations for separation, secession, self-determination and whatever name it is called are simply offshoots of the holistic failure of the Nigerian nation. The systems of government we have run and practiced over time have done little or nothing to unite us and point citizens to their greatness. Rather the selfish desire for self-perpetuation in government and in whatever high office has resulted in narrow-minded interests, emphasizing our fault lines and exploitation of religious and ethnic sentiments. A properly re-configured, reconstructed nation will provide support, solidarity, strength and security to all its constituents.

It is a historical fact that even before the amalgamation, there was trade relationship between what now constitutes geo-political regions in modern day Nigeria. There seemed to be formidable trading expeditions between northern and southern protectorates. The desire to dominate trade further led to incursions into the hinterlands leading gradually to a sort of assimilation of cultures, integration of social relationships, corporations and even the establishment of peace treaties.

All of these were before the amalgamation and so it is safe to say that the Nigerian nation first began as a trade relationship. The bravery to cross natural barriers-rivers, mountains, deserts to trade was enough demonstration of our innate desire for co-operation and interdependence. Because we are not taught the right kind of history in our schools, all of these seem obliterated from our consciousness. The basis or foundation of our nationhood is not actually accidental as some choose to believe. We have traded for centuries together and what the white man did in my view is a natural construct.

Nkem Anyata-Lafia believes we couldn't have been a nation by being Igbo alone, or just Yoruba, Hausa, Efik or Tiv. All these ethnic nationalities will bring all their unique characteristics that will help fortify and establish our nationhood.

So many things have been said about the Lugard amalgamation of 1914. Some even say it was made purely for administrative convenience of the British colonialist; Some have also said the amalgamation was intended to benefit the British solely by reducing the cost of colonial governance administration. Now the fact that the amalgamation was done without our input or interest does not mean there are to benefits derivable. Whether our coming together was accidental or a natural construct or for the sake of colonial convenience, there is an advantage in it for all of us! The beauty of our shared diversity actually makes us thick. It makes the rest of the world ponder and fear us – if we truly understand our identity and bring out the Nigerian in us.

A typical Nigerian is hardworking, a standout person, daring, courageous, god-fearing, resilient. What makes us special as Nigerians are these attributes that sometimes the foreign media tends to undermine or is afraid to admit.

Chapter **EIGHT**

A Note On Tolerance

Our multi-cultural diversity,

Plurality of our languages,

Our signature of strength to the world,

Even nature foretold our greatness.

– Osondu Chilagor

So much has been said about tolerance with so little correspondent practice in real life that I wouldn't want to indulge in an academic definition of the term. That said, the importance of tolerance should not be lost on us as we engage every day with the complexities of life's human relationships.

We have seen overtime that as societies

evolve, there comes the immanent need to have a template for tolerance particularly in a heterogeneous society like Nigeria. In this clime of close to 180 million people, there are over 200 ethnic groups, languages, cultures, and worldviews and so on. There are also political ideological and sociological differences which makes it even more complex. With all of these diversities, it is only expected that there will be fault lines. This is the void that tolerance should fill. There are always series of interacting forces pulling and exerting pressure on the fault lines such that if a culture of tolerance is not properly taught and cultivated, the result will be constant sorrow, loss and catastrophe.

In our quest to build a great nation, we need to rejig our school curriculum to have contents like tolerance taught within the context of our shared history as a people. Considering the several conflicts either religious or not we have experienced since the birth of our nation, it should be used to reflect and emphasize our unique strengths. It should also be used as a primary basis for self-acceptance. When one is able to tolerate oneself within the realm of one's capabilities and limitations, then it is easier to tolerate others. A thorough and honest self-appraisal apart from identifying one's strengths and weaknesses will help one to understand fully how he needs and depends on others.

When you are in the state where you know thyself-understanding your strengths and weaknesses, accepting genuinely your dependence on others while still being at peace with yourself, you are in a state of self-tolerance.

Self-tolerance, can easily lead to recognizing the complexity of the other person while still appreciating their contribution to our own lives. In a nation where the constituting ethnic groups are themselves self-tolerant while appreciating the difference and contributions of the other ethnic groups, there will be social harmony and economic prosperity.

Some might argue that the sheer size of our differences makes the practice of tolerance difficult if not impossible. This cannot be true because there are instances where the lack of tolerance tears apart and destroys families of just two members! And then again, there are nations like India, USA, China with higher populations mass than us who are global economic and political power houses just because they synergized their differences and adopted the principles of tolerance.

The Nigerian society must develop and implement a framework of tolerance that unifies us and focuses us to our strengths. This framework will affect political party behaviour; it will engender peace between communities, between religions, interest groups and even ideological beliefs.

It is easy to see that I have refrained from the usual name-calling that characterizes discussions on the topic of tolerance. It is deliberate. I have come to realise that whether it is the cancerous Boko Haram phenomenon, or the now perennial herdsmen-farmers clash, or the deadly communal conflicts and wars, they are all symptomic expressions of a lack of tolerance among our people. Treating the violent and virulent elements of these symptoms as government often does may at best be reactionary whereas the real peace building measures is the proactive establishment, adoption of a tolerance framework as well as the aggressive promotion of tolerance across the country. Nothing short of this will yield any positive result.

At our personal levels, there is need for us to begin to see others as complimentary and not competition. Fostering healthy relationship at the level of the individual, family, peer group, professional bodies is key to achieving our national goal as a tolerant nation.

By this, I think a clarification is required; we cannot promote tolerance for mediocrity, indolence, terrorism and other anti-social acts that are repugnant to natural justice. No. Our frame work for national tolerance, must beam the searchlight on virtues, areas of strength, unity in diversity, national productivity and every and any such thing that promotes and dignifies the Nigerian person in the eyes of the rest of the world.

Chapter **NINE**

A New Nationalism

Our rich heritage of leader-nationalists,

Resisted, impeded stoutly by ethnicity, nepotism…

Now a new breed of NIGERIANS

Propelled by patriotism.

– Osondu Chilagor

Those who lived in Herbert Macaulay, Nnamdi Azikiwe, Ahmadu Bello, Obafemi Awolowo, and Kwame Nkrumah's day will have no qualms understanding Nationalism or who a nationalist is. The nationalists are those who fought for and founded modern day Nigeria. There is no doubting the fact that they had their dreams and expectations for the new born nation. This must have spurred them to fight colonial imperialists with all they've got.

For our great nationalists, only the lowering of the union jack could stave off their patriotic desire for the emancipation of their people. They focused their mental, ideological and physical energies till the independence they fought for was gotten.

Thereafter the next tedious task was laying the foundation of the nation – Nigeria. Since most of them were young, inexperienced idealists and progressives, nothing prepared them for this humongous task of nation building. They experimented with their ideas with the obviously contagious and undeniable fuel of passion.

Their egos clashed while they ferociously contended for political space to spread their idealistic, liberal and progressive thoughts.

In some instances, they made huge mistakes as certain compromises forced the practice of politics to swallow their ideological convictions. In a bid to assert political relevance and dominance in the unending clash of egos, some retreated to their regions to at least exert unchallenged control while using it as a bargaining chip at the national level.

These unmanaged differences resulted in the creation of cult followership, whose allegiance pandered to the whims of their super-star larger-than-life heroes instead of the newly born Nigeria nation. This is the genesis of elitism, tribalism and nepotism as a brand in Nigerian politics.

Whilst an appropriate framework for the definition of Nigeria and the Nigerian has not been done, all of these faulty designs of elitism, tribalism, nepotism were dragged to the center to strangle the emerging Nigerian spirit. It was years later that we began to notice the extensive damage it has done to our civil service and our quest to be the foremost black nation in the world.

Everything in the center merely reflected how not to be a nation-the mutual suspicion, enmity and envy, lack of synergy had gone untamed.

It is even a much sadder commentary that

our great nationalists now gave birth to a breed of "ethnic Nigerians" who as foot soldiers of their hero-nationalists only watched out for what they will grab from the center to their regions. This was the anti-climax.

The plundering and corruption in the Nigeria parlance today sprang up from this point and only grew in mind-blowing proportions. Curiously enough, the faulty designs of elitism, nepotism and tribalism that attempted to short-circuit the promise of a great Nigeria nation soon, caught up with the regions and caused tensions and implosions.

Herein lies the lesson: the virtue that is required to grow and flourish the individual person is still the same that is required to make the regions and federal governments flourish. Where there is a deliberate practice and entrenchment of certain vices to peevishly undermine the center to benefit a component, even that component eventually collapses under those set of vices.

The vision and passion of our great nationalists were nearly railroaded by the greed and opportunism of the ethnic Nigerians that succeeded them. These are Nigerians whose belly and bank accounts are their measure of national pride. They pay scanty regard to national cohesion and promote crises along the national fault lines to distract attention from their excessive looting and insatiable appetite.

A new nationalism is one that will recognise the mistakes of the nationalists and the crass degeneration of the "ethnic Nigerians" that succeeded them and build a virile nation from the ruins both created. This new nationalism must have an objective at heart which is to build a great Nigerian nation, a task that must be done making use of acceptable Nigerian framework. A framework that must overcome the problem of self-definition of the Nigerian.

The new nationalists are not going to be ethnic heroes or jingoists; they must have the 'green' Nigerian blood and possess the Nigerian character. They must see the Nigerian map as their constituency – from the rainforest in the south, the grassy savannah in the north and the hilly delight and beauty of the middle-belt.

The new nationalists will be sons and daughters of Nigerian extraction who will accentuate our positions in the comity of nations as a world power and a purposefully united economic power bloc that will hold the ace in agriculture, technology, medicine, tourism, security and indeed every field of human endeavour.

A new Nationalism will create the atmosphere for the best to take up leadership positions in our nation. It will ensure the principle and practice of accountability further help cement the unity of our nation.

Chapter TEN

The Nigerian Dream: Beyond Rhetoric

---◆---

The Nigerian dream is here!

No longer an opaque, indistinguishable rhetoric.

It's happening to me.

A great nation is possible.

– Osondu Chilagor

Babatunde Raji Fashola, former Governor of Lagos State once said and I quote:

"My mother is a nurse, and my father was a journalist but the Nigerian dream has happened in my life time. It is happening here every day and the earlier we embrace it, the earlier we multiply it, the earlier we sink it down and define it and say this is what it is, that if you work hard, learn, if you are honest, you can be all that you can in the land of your ancestors. That is the Nigerian dream."

In one of my nation building series on radio, I did speak with Kingsley Bangwell, who runs a youth non-profit-Young Stars Foundation and his perspective on the issue of the Nigerian dream was quite intellectually stimulating. He argues that he does not know if there is a Nigerian dream or a general consensus of what it means or who puts it in the face of society, family or young people. Although he concedes that there is what is widely regarded as the America dream – a dream that transcends party divides, there is actually nothing in his estimation that could be readily tagged the Nigerian dream.

Governments in the past have set certain dates as vision 2000, vision 2020 all of which cannot be said to qualify for any sort of national dream. But Fashola – a visionary Nigerian and an outstanding leader appears to see a super structure from a mass of rubbles. He is able to see and define an inchoate phenomenon, and put himself forward as a beneficiary of same.

Hear him: "It is happening here every day… the earlier we sink it down and define it…"

By his pragmatic disposition, he seems to be of the view that even when there is no (at least not yet) general consensus of what the Nigerian dream is, it's existence in our everyday life is undeniable.

My fascination for the subject of the Nigerian dream grew in leaps and bounds when I examine Fashola's story of grass to grace – a testimony that assures us that opportunities abound within our country if we work hard and stay focused on our dreams. Of course, it is a telling experience that in spite of our largely unstructured and compromised system, hardwork, integrity, honesty and virtue still gets its recompense. There is still someone, some people, some system out there that appreciates integrity and hard work.

Fashola's super story of the Nigerian dream encourages us to plan our foreground since we did not choose our background. We can choose our foreground – our desired future by daring to dream; working hard, learning, honesty and the sky will be the beginning.

Fashola's clarion call for us to sink down and define the Nigerian dream is timely and a call to all Nigerians.

Heeding the call will first mean the honest acknowledgment that there are issues of despondence, disillusionment and bitterness of a failed societal system. But then, there is also that quiet but vocal promise of opportunities hidden in that perceived nemesis. There is always the guaranteed possibility of breakthrough for those who dared or cared to try. Those who seemed to ignore the whirlwind of disadvantages, negativity. Those who the sound of their dreams drowned out the noises of despair, discouragement and doubt.

All of a sudden, propelled by one's dream and the right attitude, one discovers Nigeria as a minefield of opportunities. Little wonder foreign nationals troop in in droves every day seeking the Nigerian citizenship and opportunity.

They appear to see and appreciate the

Nigerian dream better than most of us locals who are locked down and practically demobilized by the feeling of entitlement while playing the victim. We truly need to go past this victim consciousness and embrace the opportunities that so abound everywhere so that we can give life to our dreams.

Hon. Chike John Okafor – presently a Federal Lawmaker representing Obowo/Ihitte Uboma/Ehime Mbano in Imo State does earn some mention here as he also exemplifies the Nigerian dream. From a humble beginning – propelled by hard work, focus, integrity and dedication to duty, he shot up to the pinnacle of an illustrious banking profession before accepting to serve his people at the State and National levels. His was a case of the triumph of merit and virtue and more often than not, merit, does triumph irrespective of the social or even institutional limitations.

The message for my readers and particularly the youth is that there is a Nigerian dream and it is so potent and pervasive. You can literarily touch and feel it. You identify with this noble dream when you cast out the feeling of despair and take responsibility for your life. You determine that as the CEO of your life, you will not shift blames or shirk your duties to yourself. You change your mindset from that of the feeling of entitlement, dependency, guilt, brokenness and helplessness to that of a gladiator who is self-aware, and has no qualms with self-definition and whose consciousness is remoulded and perspective is changed to see only possibilities.

If you can dust yourself up and rise to the level I have just described, you are living the Nigerian dream already!

You are about to change the course of history and rewrite the history of your nation with your reformed life and actions. Congratulations.

Other BOOKS by Osondu Chilagor

Contact Information: Nigeria: +234 (0) 803 618 1037, (0) 909 430 0700

BREAKING THE SHACKLES OF THE MIND

This collection of poems beautifully intertwine past and present as a pattern for stronger belief, greater hope and deeper love in a world in search of answers.

Ter Umah – Author and Motivational Speaker

BUSINESS MORALITY IN NIGERIA: OPTION FOR NDIGBO

This book is a bold step towards widening the frontiers of business ethics. It brings to the fore the role of business ethics in fostering genuine national development.

THE CONSPIRACY

This book mirrows the traditional African Society where issues like land disputes are a common feature.

It portrays truth and justice as the only panacea for a society in dire need of reformation.

NIGHTFALL IN ZAKIBIAM

This book reminisces with pain the ugly invasion and massacre of innocent men, women and children in Benue State. It sympathizes and identifies with Benue People and Nigerians in general while reassuring the people of a brighter hope of an unfolding future.

THE VOYAGE TO NAKA

This book celebrates the TIV People of the Middle-belt of Nigeria for being dogged defenders of the soul and dignity of man in the face of excruciating lack.

TWO NIGERIANS

This is a resourceful ensemble of poems of diverse themes. The book is the portrait of a society that sails in the turbulent seas of corruption without a compass or the competent stewardship of its captain.

Printed in the United States
By Bookmasters